TULSA CITY-COUNTY LIBRARY

Sbje

TULSA CITY-COUNTY LIBRARY

D1261631

GREAT WARRIORS

BARBARIANS

VALERIE BODDEN

CREATIVE EDUCATION

Published by Creative Education
P.O. Box 227, Mankato, Minnesota 56002
Creative Education is an imprint of The Creative Company
www.thecreativecompany.us

Design by Stephanie Blumenthal
Production by Christine Vanderbeek
Art direction by Rita Marshall
Printed in the United States of America

Photographs by Alamy (color to go, INTERFOTO, Montagu Images, North Wind Picture Archives,
Photos 12), Corbis (The Print Collector), Getty Images (Bob Thomas/Popperfoto, Universal History
Archive), iStockphoto (Dimedrol68, javarman3), Shutterstock (Murat Besler), SuperStock (Pantheon)

Copyright © 2014 Creative Education
International copyright reserved in all countries. No part of this book may be reproduced
in any form without written permission from the publisher.

Library of Congress Cataloging-in-Publication Data
Bodden, Valerie.
Barbarians / Valerie Bodden.
p. cm. — (Great warriors)
Includes bibliographical references and index.
Summary: A simple introduction to the European warriors known as barbarians, including their history, life-
style, weapons, and how they remain a part of today's culture through video games and films.
ISBN 978-1-60818-466-8
1. Migrations of nations—Juvenile literature. 2. Middle Ages—Juvenile literature. 3. Military art and
science—History—Medieval, 500–1500. 4. Europe—History—392–814—Juvenile literature. I. Title.
D135.B64 2013
938—dc23   2012051833

First Edition
2 4 6 8 9 7 5 3 1

TABLE OF CONTENTS

Sometimes people fight.

They fight for food. They fight for land.

Or sometimes they fight for sport.

Barbarians were warriors who fought to

guard their land and their people.

Barbarians used many kinds of weapons

More than 2,000 years ago, people from Greece and Rome ruled much of Europe (*YOO-rup*). They called anyone who was not Greek or Roman a "barbarian." There were many different groups of barbarians. Greek and Roman armies wanted to take over the barbarians' lands. Then they wanted to make the people work for them.

VIKINGS (ABOVE) ARE CALLED "THE LAST BARBARIANS." ROMAN SOLDIERS WERE NOT KIND TO MOST BARBARIANS (BELOW).

Barbarians learned how to fight from a young age. They liked to make **ambushes**. Sometimes barbarians sent a **spy** to find out their enemy's plans.

A spy would often keep watch in a tree

Some barbarians shot stones with **slingshots**. Others used bows and arrows or swords and axes. One group hit enemies with heavy metal balls on chains.

FIGHTERS OFTEN PROTECTED THEMSELVES FROM ARROWS AND OTHER OBJECTS WITH SHIELDS.

Some barbarians fought on horses.
A group called the Goths shot bows
and arrows from carts pulled by
horses. Most barbarians wore light-
weight clothing. This helped them
move quickly and easily.

Barbarians spent a lot of time on foot or horseback

When an enemy attacked, barbarians sent their women and children to a safe place. Then they might set carts and wagons in a circle around their village. They stood behind the carts to shoot at the enemy.

A warrior did not want his wife to be in danger

SOME BARBARIANS TRAVELED BY WATER TO REACH FARAWAY LANDS. THEY SET UP NEW HOMES THERE.

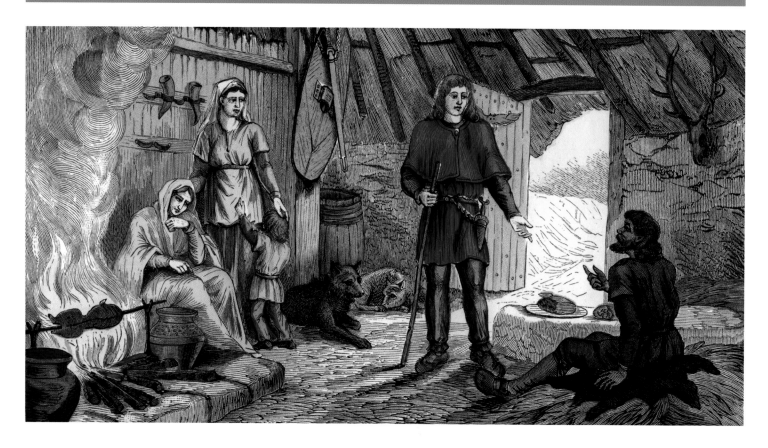

Barbarians often had to travel to do battle. They brought their women and children with them. Barbarians liked to keep their families together anytime they could.

Sometimes barbarians led attacks against the Roman **Empire**. In 410 A.D., Alaric I captured the city of Rome. Later, Attila the Hun captured more than 100 Roman cities. He killed thousands of people.

Attila the Hun scared many people

The Roman Empire ended about 1,500 years ago. After that, barbarian groups fought each other for land. Then each group found its own place to live. Barbarians did not need to battle anymore. But their stories live on in movies and video games!

CONAN THE BARBARIAN IS A POPULAR CHARACTER
IN MOVIES, BOOKS, AND VIDEO GAMES.

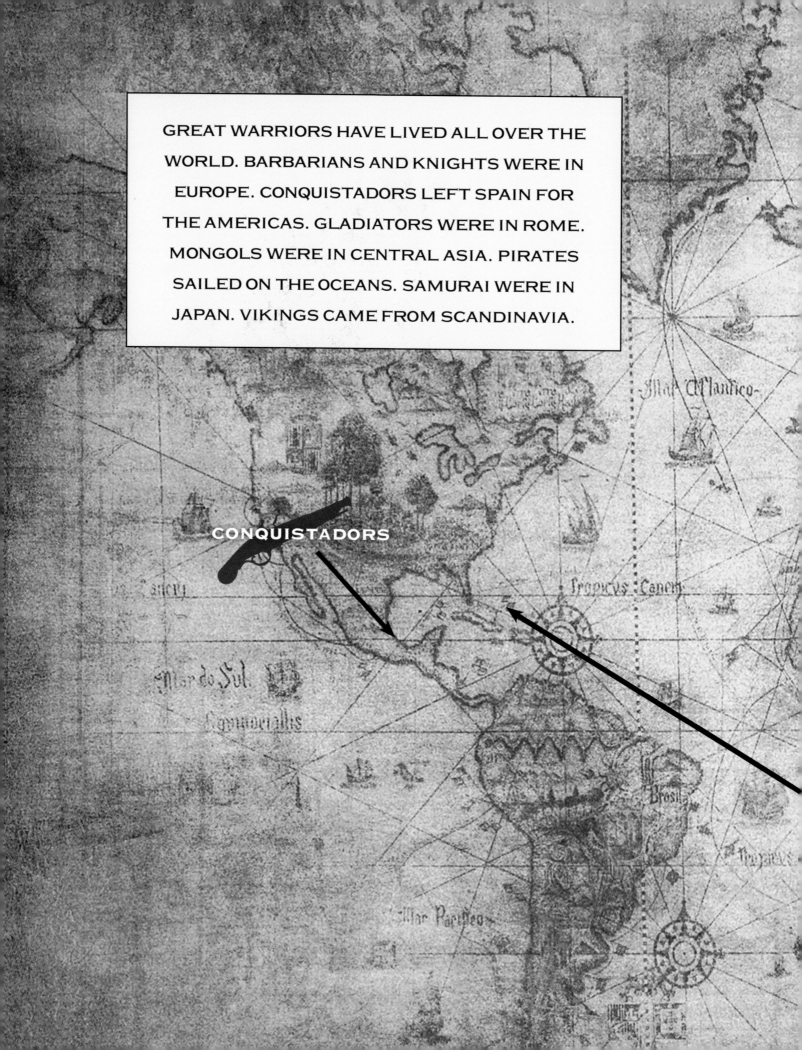

GREAT WARRIORS HAVE LIVED ALL OVER THE WORLD. BARBARIANS AND KNIGHTS WERE IN EUROPE. CONQUISTADORS LEFT SPAIN FOR THE AMERICAS. GLADIATORS WERE IN ROME. MONGOLS WERE IN CENTRAL ASIA. PIRATES SAILED ON THE OCEANS. SAMURAI WERE IN JAPAN. VIKINGS CAME FROM SCANDINAVIA.

CONQUISTADORS

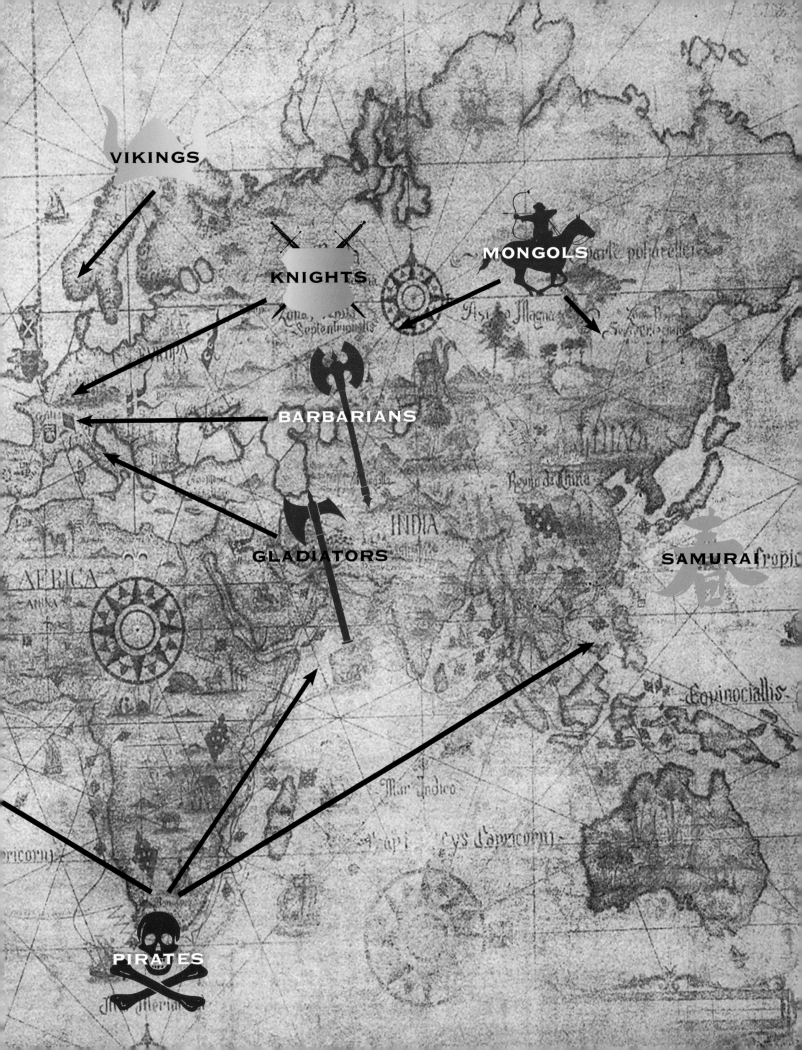

GLOSSARY

ambushes—attacks made by hiding and then surprising the enemy

empire—many lands that are ruled by one leader

slingshots—weapons made from a strap attached to a stick shaped like a Y and used to fling stones through the air

spy—a person who secretly watches what someone else is doing so that he or she can report it to others

READ MORE

Fullman, Joe. *Celts: Dress, Eat, Write and Play Just Like the Celts*. Mankato, Minn.: QEB, 2010.

Pratt, Leonie. *Celts*. London: Usborne, 2007.

INDEX